ALANA VALENTINE's writing was nominated for two Helpmann Awards, including best New Australian Work and Best Play, for *Parramatta Girls* (2007). Most recently her play about Afghan/Australian Muslim women, *Shafana and Aunt Sarrina: Soft Revolution*, was honoured with a 2009 Sydney Theatre Awards nomination in the Best Independent Production category and her play *The Modest Aussie Cozzie*, based on the life of *burquini* creator Aheda Zanetti, was part of the Riverview Cultural Festival in 2009.

Alana is the recipient of a 2010/11 Literature Fund Fellowship from the Australia Council, the 2004 Queensland Premier's Award for Best Drama Script, a 2003 NSW Writer's Fellowship, the 2002 Rodney Seaborn Playwrights' Award, and an International Writing Fellowship at Shakespeare's Globe Theatre in London. She has also received two AWGIE Awards, a Victorian Green Room Award nomination, a 2001 commendation for the Louis Esson Prize, a residency at the Banff Playwrights' Conference in Canada, the ANPC/New Dramatists Award in New York, a Churchill Fellowship, a Centenary Medal and a NSW Premier's Award.

Alana's stage plays include *Lost Illusions* (2010), *Head Full of Love* (2010), *Watermark* (2008), *Eyes to the Floor* (2008), *Singing the Lonely Heart* (2006), *Run Rabbit Run* (2004) and *Savage Grace* (2003).

In 2001 Alana was the recipient of a Graduate Diploma in Museum Studies (with Merit) from the University of Sydney and has created Museum Theatre works for the Museum of Sydney, Australian National Maritime Museum, Australian War Memorial, Sydney Jewish Museum, Hyde Park Barracks Museum and Sydney Observatory.

Camilla Ah Kin (left) as Sarrinah and Sheridan Harbridge as Shafana in the 2009 Alex Buzo Company production in Sydney. (Photo: Heidrun Löhr)

SHAFANA & AUNT SARRINAH

soft revolution

ALANA VALENTINE

CURRENCY PRESS
SYDNEY

CURRENCY PLAYS

First published in 2010
by Currency Press Pty Ltd,
PO Box 2287, Strawberry Hills, NSW, 2012, Australia
enquiries@currency.com.au
www.currency.com.au

COPYING FOR EDUCATIONAL PURPOSES

The Australian *Copyright Act 1968* (Act) allows a maximum of one chapter or 10% of this book, whichever is the greater, to be copied by any educational institution for its educational purposes provided that that educational institution (or the body that administers it) has given a remuneration notice to Copyright Agency Limited (CAL) under the Act.

For details of the CAL licence for educational institutions contact CAL, Level 15/233 Castlereagh Street, Sydney, NSW, 2000; tel: within Australia 1800 066 844 toll free; outside Australia 61 2 9394 7600; fax: 61 2 9394 7601; email: info@copyright.com.au

COPYING FOR OTHER PURPOSES

Except as permitted under the Act, for example a fair dealing for the purposes of study, research, criticism or review, no part of this book may be reproduced, stored in a retrieval system, or transmitted in any form or by any means without prior written permission. All enquiries should be made to the publisher at the address above.

Any performance or public reading of *Shafana and Aunt Sarrinah: Soft Revolution* is forbidden unless a licence has been received from the author or the author's agent. The purchase of this book in no way gives the purchaser the right to perform the plays in public, whether by means of a staged production or reading. All applications for public performance should be addressed to RGM, PO Box 128 Surry Hills, 2010, NSW, Australia; phone: 61 2 9281 3911; email: info@rgm.com.au

NATIONAL LIBRARY OF AUSTRALIA CIP DATA

Author:	Valentine, Alana, 1961–.
Title:	Shafana and Aunt Sarrinah: soft revolution / Alana Valentine.
ISBN:	9780868198828 (pbk.)
Subjects:	Hijab (Islamic clothing)–Australia–Drama.
	Muslim women–Australia–Social conditions–Drama.
Dewey Number: A822.3	

Typeset by Dean Nottle for Currency Press.
Printed by Hyde Park Press, Richmond, SA.
Cover illustration and design by Emma Vine for Currency Press.

Contents

Creating Identity in a Hostile World
    Christina Ho   *vii*

Shafana and Aunt Sarrinah: A Reflection
    Makiz Ansari   *xiii*

SHAFANA AND AUNT SARRINAH: SOFT REVOLUTION   1

Camilla Ah Kin (left) as Sarrinah and Sheridan Harbridge as Shafana in the 2009 Alex Buzo Company production in Sydney. (Photo: Heidrun Löhr)

Creating Identity in a Hostile World

As I'm writing this, Australia is embroiled in the latest round of the 'hijab debates'—those regular, often hysterical arguments over whether we should ban the hijab or burqa, whether Muslim women are enslaved by their religion, and whether 'Australian values' are being irreparably damaged by excessive multiculturalism.

In these debates, the hijab is typically reduced to a symbol of oppression, a garment that obliterates the individuality and free will of the Muslim woman, that signals her second-class status in relation to men, and that renders her a powerless victim of a barbaric religion. For the sake of equality and women's rights, we should ban the hijab—or so the argument goes.

Amongst these histrionics, *Shafana and Aunt Sarrinah: Soft Revolution* is a quietly insightful intervention that portrays what the media headlines never can: the multiple meanings of the hijab for Muslim women. In contrast to the singular meaning given to the hijab in public debates, Alana Valentine's play powerfully shows that the hijab has many meanings: it is about faith, politics, liberation, identity, and each woman's personal history as a Muslim.

In contrast to the binary debate in the media, framed as a clash between Islam and the West, *Shafana and Aunt Sarrinah* portrays the passionate debates within Islam between devout Muslims who may profoundly disagree. One woman's liberation is another's oppression. Shafana's 'superman cape' is Sarrinah's suffocating 'tent'. Shafana's religious ecstasy is, to Sarrinah, dangerous fanaticism. These debates are going on daily in kitchens, over meals, in local gatherings, between Muslims everywhere confronting difficult decisions. Yet in the national imaginary, Muslims are simply a monolithic bloc of trenchant opposition to 'Western values'.

And ironically the more 'hijab debates' we have in the public sphere, the less we actually hear about what ordinary Muslims in Australia might really think about the hijab, or any other issue that has been polarised between 'oppressive Islam' and 'enlightened West'. The more 'hijab debates' we have, the more Muslim communities are cornered into defending Islam, including the hijab, at all costs. The space for free and unfettered internal debate where Muslims explore the complexities, contradictions and nuances of their faith and identity is in danger of disappearing. In a climate in which Muslims feel under siege, any dissent from the 'official line'—usually articulated by a conservative male religious leader—can be read as a betrayal of the community.

Muslim women, in particular, may feel unable to speak out about sexism or violence within their own community for fear of fuelling the already raging fire that brands Islam as oppressive, and Muslim men as barbaric. The result, then, can be a reductive hardening of Muslims' own representation of themselves, and of Islam. The hijab, in particular, can be seen as a mark of Muslim authenticity, rendering unveiled women 'less Islamic'. The Muslim feminist writer Shakira Hussein expresses it succinctly:

> As someone who has spoken out against 'anti-hijab' voices such as Bronwyn Bishop and Leslie Cannold I face a dilemma: how do I defend women's right to wear hijab, free from discrimination and harassment, without also reinforcing the position of hijab as a symbol of 'real' Muslim womanhood, which I have no desire to do?
>
> (Hussein 2007: 5)

As *Shafana and Aunt Sarrinah* eloquently shows, there will always be multiple interpretations of the hijab among Muslim women. Valentine gives us a glimpse of the fiercely contested meanings and powerful convictions that can painfully divide family members who nonetheless maintain a deep love for one another.

Shafana and Aunt Sarrinah also shows how the 'hijab decision' can never be just a personal expression of faith, even when that is what a woman desperately wishes. As Sarrinah tells Shafana, a veiled Muslim woman turns herself into a symbol, 'an endless advertisement that says "Ask me", "Accuse me"'. She will need a ready response for any number of questions about the Bali bombings, Middle Eastern wars, 9/11, the Taliban, honour killings and so on and on and on. In Australia it has been well documented by the Human Rights Commission and others that veiled women bore the brunt of attacks against Muslims after 9/11, including having their hijabs ripped off their heads (HREOC 2004). The meanings of the veil are therefore not only multiple, but overwhelmingly beyond the control of the women who wear it. In this sense the 'hijab debates' have almost entirely hijacked the hijab itself, imposing external imperatives that preclude its interpretation as a pure act of personal faith.

It should be noted, however, that this is nothing new. The practice of veiling has always been somewhat overdetermined by the social context in which wearers find themselves. Since colonial days the veil has been constructed as a symbol of oppression. For British and French colonial governments in Egypt, Algeria, India and elsewhere, the veil indicated the backwardness of colonised peoples. Those who did not know 'how to treat women properly' were undeserving of self-governance—even though at this time women in Europe did not have the vote. And as Leila Ahmed documents in her superb history, *Women and Gender in Islam*, Lord Cromer, the British Consul-General of Egypt (1883–1907), who named the poor treatment of women as the foremost evidence of the 'complete failure' of Islam as a social system, was, back in Britain in 1919, a founding member and President of the Men's League for Opposing Woman Suffrage (Ahmed 1992: 152–153).

Naturally, many Muslim women responded to such attacks on the hijab with a renewed commitment to it and, for some, veiling became an expression of political and national affiliations, including anti-colonial and anti-Western sentiments. In the twentieth century the 'new veiling' in the Islamic world can be traced to the 1967 and 1973 wars with Israel (MacLeod 1992: 541). Post-9/11, many women have again taken up the hijab as an expression of their identity and as a sign of solidarity with their fellow Muslims. For many, becoming visibly Muslim is a political statement as much as a religious one, a rejection of defensive strategies of assimilation or anonymity in favour of an active assertion of identity.

In this highly charged environment it is not surprising that it is Shafana rather than her aunt who makes the controversial decision to wear the hijab. One outcome of the post-9/11 era has been a generation of young Muslims who are particularly mobilised by their faith. Having grown up in the shadow of the War on Terror, Islam has not been a neutral part of young Muslims' identities in the way that religion might be for others. Being Muslim is something they have had to constantly explain and defend, and therefore work out clearly for themselves. In the process, there has been a well-documented 'Islamic reassertion' among many young Muslims around the world. Contrary to previous trends that have seen the children of migrants assimilate into the social and cultural life of mainstream society, in the face of racism and Islamophobia many young Muslims have embraced a religious identity that deliberately distinguishes itself from 'mainstream' practices and values.

The wearing of the hijab is one obvious manifestation of this religious reassertion. While Western 'hijab debaters' perpetrate moral panic about Muslim women being oppressed by conservative families and communities, in fact it is often a case of young women defying the wishes of their families in deciding to wear the hijab. Shafana's experience mirrors the stories of young Muslim women around the world who depart from the practice of their unveiled mothers and aunts, and put on the hijab in the face of their opposition. Like so many other young Muslims in the post-9/11 era, Shafana turns to faith to create a strong sense of her own identity in a hostile world. She embraces that which would be used against her by others and redeploys it as a source of strength.

I have nothing but admiration for young women like Shafana, whose strength of conviction enables them to wear the hijab in full knowledge of the challenges this will bring to their daily lives. Alongside this admiration however is a deep sense of injustice that such a decision should have to become so difficult and so fraught with risk—not only to these young women's personal safety and wellbeing, but to their most intimate relationships with loved ones. Wearing a hijab should not be a symbol of anything that a woman does not wish it to be. Especially in a multicultural society such as Australia, a decision to put on the hijab should be an act that is unremarkable and unremarked upon, just another expression of identity amongst thousands, from the wearing of crucifixes to Converse sneakers. It should not be subject to the kind of frenzied public debate we have witnessed in this country of late, the kind of debate that dramatically shrinks the opportunities for ordinary Shafanas and Sarinnahs to make personal choices with freedom and dignity.

References

Ahmed, L. 1992 *Women and gender in Islam: Historical roots of a modern debate*, New Haven: Yale University Press.

HREOC (Human Rights and Equal Opportunity Commission) 2004 *Ismae— Listen: National consultations on eliminating prejudice against Arab and Muslim Australians*, HREOC.

Hussein, S. 2007 'The limits of force/choice discourses in discussing Muslim women's dress codes' *Transforming Cultures eJournal*, 2(1) http://epress.lib. uts.edu.au/ojs/index.php/TfC/article/view/612 (accessed 7 October, 2010).

MacLeod, A. E. 1992 'Hegemonic Relations and Gender Resistance: The new veiling as accommodating protest in Cairo', *Signs* 17(3): 533–557.

Christina Ho
Sydney, 2010

Dr Christina Ho is a Senior Lecturer at the Faculty of Arts and Social Sciences, University of Technology, Sydney. She researches migration, multiculturalism and the politics of diversity, focusing particularly on the experiences of Muslim Australians and the Chinese diaspora. She is the co-editor of *Beyond the Hijab Debates: New Conversations on Gender, Race and Religion*, Cambridge Scholars Publishing, 2009.

Sheridan Harbridge as Shafana in the 2009 Alex Buzo Company production in Sydney. (Photo: Heidrun Löhr)

Shafana and Aunt Sarrinah: A Reflection

It was a profound experience to meet Alana Valentine for the first time. Her depth of understanding and receptiveness became a mirror for me to view the pages of my own story as I reflected over my inner spiritual journey through undulating terrains of life. That evening I began telling the story of a young Australian Muslim girl with an Afghan background.

Unfortunately the usual sensational coverage of Muslims makes us approach any media involvement with caution. But I trusted Alana's intention as an authentic attempt to understand my hybrid outer identity and the way my spiritual journey played out within my family. I became confident that Alana's approach (as well as that of the Alex Buzo Company) differed from the sensationalism of many others and therefore I saw an opportunity to voice an Australian Muslim's experience seldom heard. This, I hoped, might serve my fellow Australians as a genuine contribution towards better understanding.

At the same time, I found comfort in sharing a story which I hoped would resonate universally. This was a look at the inner life and its quest for higher realities. Cultural differences are usually visible, yet inner quests may not be. I wanted to share my inner journey with those who are willing to explore beyond the headscarf.

Nevertheless, in August 2009 I was not sure what to expect as I went to watch the production of *Shafana and Aunt Sarrinah* with my aunt and some family members. I was unsure how it would turn out or how my aunt would receive it. Would it be confronting in any way? Mixed feelings and thoughts circled my mind as I made my way towards the Seymour Centre. The first play of the night, *Norm and Ahmed* put forth a gripping depiction of migrant experiences. When *Shafana and Aunt Sarrinah* began after the interval, I began to see certain pages of my life unfold before me. Wow—there I was sitting on the chair and watching the conversation between a niece and her aunt who had conflicting approaches towards spiritual journeys; scenes still fresh on the screen of my memories. I saw the suffocating cultural hurt from the past and the stereotypes of the present that had coalesced to distance an aunt from her niece. Fear of the unknown had alarmed Aunt Sarrinah who pleads with Shafana to stay away from her daughter.

What had come between the close family and disrupted this friendship was more than a piece of cloth. For the aunt it was a symbol—the reminder of dreaded experiences of the Afghan culture that wore the garb of Muslim identity and what it represented in her mind. This lacked in its essence the inner wisdom and spirit which Shafana discovered in her university years in Australia, a reality that is ever alive in my consciousness. Such ironies of culture and religion and the large grey zone between them had set off my quest for meaningful certitude on one hand, while on the other, the intellectual battle against the shock of September Eleven propelled me to explore the integrity of Islam as a faith system with an ability to instil in its followers inner peace. Watching the play reminded me such background and confirmed for me some poignant themes:

• At the outset there was a clear generational gap. I think that youth are too often perceived to have overriding emotions which take away from their foresight and ability to make positive choices in life. The play was an experiential confirmation of this feeling. The generational gaps can be deeper when it has an overlay of cultural gaps. Older people in migrant communities have received a different education and life experience to the younger people who have Australian education and a life experience concretely set in Australian time and space.

• Hearing Shafana and Aunt Sarrinah use some Persian words highlighted the strong role that language plays in the communication of ideas and self expression. This deepens the generational gap for the bi-lingual and multi-lingual. Certain concepts carry with it negative associations. *Chador*, the Persian word for headscarf, may have a spiritual meaning for Shafana. Yet to her Aunt Sarrinah it can be an expression of submissiveness to the patriarchal society where strength of muscles may rule over reason and be deemed superior.

• Human nature is not homogenous. Within the same family, unique understandings and appreciations can exist. For this reason, personal values can be relative, contingent on age, social conditioning and character disposition. The depiction of frustration between Shafana and her aunt captured something that was true in my own life.

During the interval, before *Shafana and Aunt Sarinnah* started, my aunt's facial expressions conveyed mixed messages. We did not talk about the play. I could only guess what was going through her mind. Was she able to see the zoomed-out picture and now understood me and my choices? Was her discomfort a personal one with me only or was she looking through me with other associations? Do we only view our choices in life through the prisms of extremism, rebelliousness and a defiance of family norms?

As the play progressed the expressions on my aunt took a clearer shape as I sensed a nod of approval. At the end I read the smile on her face as an assurance that she understood my choices in my own frame of reference. I was not rebelling against my family or culture; my actions were neither a political statement nor an outward demonstration of identity. They were more than all these things. They were about my own inner journey and reflection of my convictions as an independent Muslim woman.

I am glad and hopeful that my conversation with Alana Valentine that first evening has given rise to an Australian story seldom told.

Makiz Ansari
Sydney, 2010

Makiz Ansari has been active in inter-faith and inter-cultural dialogue. She served as the Director and Education Co-ordinator for the Affinity Intercultural Foundation. Makiz is currently the Director and Education Co-ordinator at the Islamic Sciences and Research Academy of Australia.

ACKNOWLEDGEMENTS

This play is a work of fiction, but I hope that it echoes the stories and opinions told to me by a cross-section of Australian Muslim women. They include Katie el Hakim, Halme Kilciler, Houda El Ri Fain, Ilhelm, Fadila Zaney, Fatima, Raisa, Harima and Zowet from Cumberland House, Zuleyhe Seyfi Seyit, Lalia Daqiq, and, especially, Makiz Ansari, from the Affinity Intercultural Foundation. I also spoke to and thank Maha, Nuha, Amani, Nada and Fatima Mawas from the Muslim Womens' Association, Ruby Kargarian and several others who wish to remain anonymous. Thanks also to Sadaf Kohistani for her expert assistance with the written word Dari. The Literature Fund of the Australia Council provided me with an Established Writers Grant which facilitated a large part of the research on the project and the Sidney Myer Foundation generously provided funding to the Buzo Company to commission the play.

Shafana and Aunt Sarrinah: Soft Revolution was first produced by the Alex Buzo Company at the Seymour Centre, Sydney, on 5 August 2009, with the following cast:

SHAFANA	Sheridan Harbridge
SARRINAH	Camilla Ah Kin

Director, Aarne Neeme
Designer, Deirdre Burges
Lighting, Tony Youlden

CHARACTERS

SHAFANA

SARRINAH, her aunt

SHAFANA *is in a laboratory, surrounded by jars of creatures in preserving solution. She is rehearsing a speech, half to her aunt, half to the audience.*

SHAFANA: You get to a point, okay, why don't I be honest, you get to an age and you've absorbed so much and you've observed so much, that you think that you know, basically, what the world has to offer. You've seen it all. Or at least variations of it all. And it's not that you're tired or arrogant or lazy, although they're not the worst things you can be. It's a survival thing. If you're smart and if you've been through a lot, and who hasn't, you can at least congratulate yourself on your ability to vaguely see what might be coming next. To be able to predict situations and not be disorientated. Oh, you don't mind being pleasantly surprised. But you don't like to be caught entirely off guard. It's what separates successful people from other people, isn't it? Foresight. And you work at it too, at 'keeping up' and 'keeping in touch' because if you do, you're not going to be fooled. You've sussed out most probabilities so you're ahead of the game. Which is canny.

But there always comes a point where you lose it. Where a whole generation lose touch. They start to listen to what looks like the next thing. It sounds like the next thing and it acts like that next thing but it's not the next thing. The truly astonishing thing about what's coming next is that it's nothing like what this generation were like, old or young. It's utterly unfamiliar.

If you're a scientist you have to guard against false assumptions. You've all heard the cliché about having to recognise the veil of knowing and surrender to unknowing. But knowing or thinking you know the answers is only one veil. There are others, like physical barriers to seeing. We still don't know half of what is in the deep, deep oceans because they're veiled with darkness. But the creatures are there. Growing, changing, like nothing we've ever seen before. To be discovered. Like the future. Which is not just veiled by time but also by the eyes we're looking at it with. Yes?

What if I told you that in the future you might make a choice that today, right now, you would utterly deny. What if I told you that a change is coming, for you, that is so unbelievable that it would make you laugh out loud if I mentioned it.

SARRINAH *enters.*

But believe me, believe me, there are yet new worlds to be fathomed and new impossibilities to be revealed.

SARRINAH: Shafana.

SHAFANA: In the vast undersea there are vents which scientists call black smokers.

SARRINAH: Are you ready?

SHAFANA: Two thousand five hundred metres down, clouds of pluming black particles are belched into the sea, coughed out like clouds of choking fumes, and four hundred degrees Celsius hot.

SARRINAH: And I'm interested in this why?

SHAFANA: This is molten quartz, studded with iron, copper, zinc, nickel and hydrogen sulphide.

SARRINAH: If you said it was liquid chocolate, studded with sultanas, pistachio, and pieces of orange rind you'd get my attention faster.

SHAFANA: As this metallic cocktail shrieks out into the cold sea water, the ferric sulphide turns black and it appears as if, fantastically, gusts of glossy black air are puffing through the water.

SARRINAH: Just as great gusts of indifference will be glazing over the eyes of your tutorial participants.

SHAFANA: You told me I should use images, try to paint a picture when I give my presentations.

SARRINAH: You could turn the dial up a little more on your best David Attenborough.

SHAFANA: Now, through the miasma of this vaporous haze we have begun to find creatures.

SARRINAH: Come on, leave your vaporous haze where it is and come with me.

SHAFANA: But I'm getting to the best bit.

SARRINAH: Go on then.

SHAFANA: Riftia pachyptila, a giant tube worm, fills out to its full length of one and a half metres in less than two years, without a mouth and without a gut. How can it grow if it does not eat in any observable way? It allows itself to be covered in bacteria, crawling with it, swarming with it, and is sustained by the hydrogen sulphide that they secrete. An enormous, snake-like worm that does not consume or excrete.

SARRINAH: So, no fun at a party.

Sheridan Harbridge as Shafana in the 2009 Alex Buzo Company production in Sydney. (Photo: Heidrun Löhr)

SHAFANA: But don't you think that's amazing?

SARRINAH: I think if you start your presentation with so many facts you're in danger of losing them.

SHAFANA: But how about you, don't *you* think that's incredible?

SARRINAH: A worm that does not eat or shit? Yeah. Why not. Whoopee. Let's just all say worm poo, worm poo, worm poo in quick succession.

SHAFANA: For millions of small shrimp, daily life is an extreme sport, balanced as they are on the edge of a steaming hot, poisonous soup that threatens in an instant to consume, cook or toxify them. And yet they thrive in colonies of thousands and thousands.

SARRINAH: Life can perversely defy expectations.

SHAFANA: Yes. Exactly. These are creatures unknown to science, resistant to reason, oppositional to logic and there are, doubtless, many more to be found.

SARRINAH: Yes, but your fellow students don't care about that. The secret to a good tutorial presentation is to ease your listeners in gradually, talk to them about the people who set out to find these black smokers, the difficulties of funding their expedition, the dangers to them of going down to the ocean depths. Then once they are interested in the human story, then hit them with the facts.

SHAFANA: Why are you being so critical?

SARRINAH: You wanted me to give you feedback.

SHAFANA: I've just found the way to start.

SARRINAH: Of all the steps the first is the one that challenges us most.

SHAFANA: Is that an ancient Persian saying?

SARRINAH: No, it was on a flyer advertising my local gym.

SHAFANA: Oh, Aunt.

SARRINAH: Well it was.

SHAFANA: It's a difficult subject to explain.

SARRINAH: What's difficult? There are all these wormy little wrigglers swimming around unable to see anymore because they've all been blinded by the lights of investigating submarines.

She closes her eyes and stumbles around the space.

SHAFANA: They discovered species with white eyes suffered more damage than those with pink eyes.

SARRINAH: Fine. So you say in your tutorial that down there it's cook or be cooked.

SHAFANA: You think like an engineer.

SARRINAH: I am an engineer. I'm a doctor of engineering.

SHAFANA: I know that.

SARRINAH: Yes, but now you can believe it.

SHAFANA: Because it will say so on your ID card.

SARRINAH: Because it will say so on my ID card and until it does I am Sarrinah Obaidullah, Afghani migrant and nobody.

SHAFANA: No you're not.

SARRINAH: Believe me when I say that I am and that's why we need to get over there to get this done.

SHAFANA: I'm on a roll.

SARRINAH: You don't want to see your Aunt become a doctor?

SHAFANA: You're already that. You've been that for ten years.

SARRINAH: And you know very well that in Australia I have not been that.

SHAFANA: You got them to recognise your qualifications.

SARRINAH: But these have an Aussie flavour, Miss Worm Poo. [*Pause.*] Come on. You said that you needed to get your student card renewed. We can do it at the same time.

SHAFANA: This is worth forty percent of my mark.

>   *Pause.*

SARRINAH: When is your tutorial presentation?

SHAFANA: Tomorrow afternoon.

SARRINAH: Well, this should only take ten minutes. All they have to do is take the photos and then laminate the cards. You'll be in and out of there.

SHAFANA: I think I'd rather keep going.

SARRINAH: You won't get another appointment for a week.

SHAFANA: I rang them. They can fit me in tomorrow.

SARRINAH: You rang them. When?

SHAFANA: Before.

>   *Pause.*

SARRINAH: Okay then. You've had your fun. I know you're teasing me.

SHAFANA: I'm not.

SARRINAH: I know you are. Because my faculty is on the opposite side of the campus. I had to walk all the way across and now I have to walk all the way back. You think I like walking? I hate walking in this heat.

I get hot. I won't have a drink of water because it's Ramadan and I am fasting. And unlike your slimy little tamale worms I don't want to spend my life coated in a near-death bouillabaisse of perspiration.

SHAFANA: I wanted you to hear my presentation.

SARRINAH: Incredible vents and impossible creatures.

Pause.

SHAFANA: I want to talk to you about something.

SARRINAH: What?

SHAFANA: The truly horrifying thing about what's coming next is that it's nothing like what this generation were like, old or young. It's utterly unfamiliar.

SARRINAH: Which is why we have Google.

SHAFANA: What?

SARRINAH: Search engines. Modern version of a crystal ball.

SHAFANA: That's not what I'm talking about.

SARRINAH: If it can't be found on Google you've got to wonder how relevant your vision really is.

Pause.

SHAFANA: Let me come round to your place to eat.

SARRINAH: When?

SHAFANA: Why, what, when? Could you be a little bit more understanding?

SARRINAH: Understanding? What's wrong?

SHAFANA: Nothing. I just want to have a meal and… you know… have a chat.

SARRINAH: Tell me right now what is wrong with you.

SHAFANA: Aunt. I'm fine.

SARRINAH: Does your mother know? [*Beat.*] Are you taking drugs?

SHAFANA: What? No.

SARRINAH: I see Muslims in the paper snorting cocaine.

SHAFANA: I'm not snorting cocaine.

SARRINAH: They could at least stick to opium. Support the Taliban's cash crop of choice.

SHAFANA: That's not funny.

SARRINAH: Not at all funny. But I know that you are not taking drugs. Like you are not having sex. [*Beat.*] Are you?

SHAFANA: Of course not.

SARRINAH: Are you scared of your sexuality?

SHAFANA: What?

SARRINAH: I was. I used to lie on my bed praying for bigger boobs and when I got them I was horrified. Of the effect they had on other people. Suddenly you have to enter into this hierarchy of desirability. Terrifying. There's a lot to be scared of whether you're... or not.

SHAFANA: I... don't want to talk about this.

SARRINAH: So tell me.

SHAFANA: Aunt, please. Tonight. We will break our fast together. Go and get your ID card. I'm sorry I can't come with you but I'll see it tonight.

> *Pause.*

SARRINAH: You really aren't going to come with me?

SHAFANA: I want to get a good mark. I need to get a good mark.

SARRINAH: Sure.

> *Pause.* SHAFANA *struggles.*

SHAFANA: I've hurt you.

SARRINAH: Don't be silly.

SHAFANA: I have.

SARRINAH: No, I understand, concentrate on your studies. That's good.

SHAFANA: I've really hurt you.

SARRINAH: The cat's witness is its tail.

SHAFANA: What?

SARRINAH: It's an old Persian saying.

> *Pause.*

SHAFANA: I'll see you tonight.

> SARRINAH *leaves.* SHAFANA *speaks to the audience.*

I was born in Afghanistan. In Kabul. I was quite young when I left the country, and at the time I left the Russians were withdrawing from Afghanistan. I have two other sisters and a brother. So there's four of us altogether. It was 1989. And so we came to India and in India... we stayed until 1994. In New Delhi. I was the first one to come to Australia. My aunt and uncle were already here. I was fourteen years old and went straight into high school.

> *Flashback 1994. The aunt's home.*

SARRINAH: You want me to come as a pear?

SHAFANA: Do I what?

SARRINAH: Do you wanting me to come to school as a pear?

SHAFANA: A pair of what?

SARRINAH: Not a pair of what, that is a pair like a pair of socks, yes?

SHAFANA: Aunt, just say it in Dari.

SARRINAH: No, if I come to the school as a pear, I must speak in English.

SHAFANA: So what the hell is a pear?

SARRINAH: Don't be saying hell. I know the bad words first.

SHAFANA: Sure.

SARRINAH: A pear. To speak to the teachers.

SHAFANA: What the bloody hell is a pear?

> SARRINAH *holds her finger out to her.*

SARRINAH: For now. For until your mother and father come to Australia you stay with me and I am the pear.

> *Pause.*

SHAFANA: The parent.

SARRINAH: Ah. The pear-ant.

SHAFANA: -ent.

SARRINAH: Par-unt.

SHAFANA: Right.

SARRINAH: The par-unt and teacher day. To this I am coming.

SHAFANA: Whatever.

SARRINAH: Shafana?

SHAFANA: You can't even speak properly.

SARRINAH: I was not so long in India as your family.

SHAFANA: I know.

SARRINAH: We were accepted much faster.

SHAFANA: Yeah, so why come if you can't speak?

SARRINAH: You don't want me to come to see the teacher?

> *Beat.*

SHAFANA: No. I don't.

SARRINAH: Why?

SHAFANA: Just. Just wait till you get your qualifications… accepted.

SARRINAH: My engineering degree.

SHAFANA: Yes.

SARRINAH: Why?

SHAFANA: Well, what are you going to tell the teacher? That you work in a factory now? [*Pause.*] She says, 'Hello Mrs Obaidullah and what is it you do?', and you say, 'I work packing hardware supplies'?

SARRINAH: In Kabul I am the chief engineer at the academy.

SHAFANA: Yeah, so what?

SARRINAH: So what? This is what you think of me?

SHAFANA: It's not what I think of you, it's what's true. You work in a factory and this is what you read.

> *She takes a magazine out of* SARRINAH'*s handbag.*

Is this the engineering journal for Australia? No.

> SARRINAH *tries to get the magazine back.*

Who Weekly?

SARRINAH: You don't understand.

SHAFANA: You know what? You're right. The Aunt Sarrinah I knew would never read *Who Weekly.*

SARRINAH: The other women who I am working with, they are doing to talk about celebrities and weight problems.

SHAFANA: *Who Weekly.*

SARRINAH: Stop saying *Who Weekly.*

SHAFANA: So. You don't have to lower yourself to their level.

SARRINAH: I want to fit in. Not to be too unusual.

SHAFANA: You don't have to do that.

SARRINAH: I need to making friends, Shafana.

SHAFANA: You don't want to be friends with such women.

SARRINAH: I am such women.

SHAFANA: They are not educated.

SARRINAH: Why do you say such women?

SHAFANA: Because they don't want to be educated.

SARRINAH: Not everyone can be educated.

SHAFANA: Yes, they can. In this country they can.

SARRINAH: No, that is not—

SHAFANA: Such women want to talk about diets and gossip all their life. They are given everything and they pour it away like rubbish. They have so many choices and they waste their minds. [*Pause.*] My teachers won't know that you were an engineer. All they'll see is your rough hands and tired eyes and—

SARRINAH: But they can see you are smart.

SHAFANA: Yes, but if you turn up, spluttering and stuttering and working in a factory.

SARRINAH: They will think less of you?

SHAFANA: It's just easier if they don't… see you, like that.

Pause.

SARRINAH: Who will come to the pear-unt night with you?

SHAFANA: I don't have to go. It's optional.

Pause.

SARRINAH: I will be getting them to recognise my degree.

SHAFANA: I hope so.

SARRINAH: Soon. I will be working again in building.

SHAFANA: Yeah. Maybe.

> SARRINAH *is in her kitchen, surrounded by jars of preserved food. She holds the jar up to the light and speaks as if she is on camera. She goes into a Nigella Lawson impersonation that is uncannily convincing… all the head tossing and pouting.*

SARRINAH: Let's talk about long grain rice… in the Afghan way of cooking we use big, succulent pieces of rice that you can really get your mouth around and we cook it in such a way that you get rid of all that nasty starch. That's right. Take every shortcut you can, cooking is about relaxation. Ooh, now look at that rice, all that gorgeous puffiness and saltiness will mix with the meat for the pilau. I use brown rice because it has that lovely nutty flavour. You could slice up a sweet little onion because of the nice crunchy texture in your mouth. Nyum nyum nyum.

> SHAFANA *enters.*

SHAFANA: What are you doing?

SARRINAH: [*still as Nigella*] Or use leeks. I've found a supermarket where they are already washed and peeled because, even though peeling an onion is not that hard, it can seem terribly tiring sometimes.

SHAFANA: Why are you talking out loud like that, as if you are conducting a cooking class?

SARRINAH: I'm practising.

SHAFANA: For what?

SARRINAH: Don't you tell me you haven't been prancing around in front of a mirror. You and your Bollywood dance moves.

> SARRINAH *does a Bollywood-style dance with* SHAFANA.

SHAFANA: I have not.

SARRINAH: You told me you love Bollywood movies.

SHAFANA: I do. Doesn't mean I want to be in one.

SARRINAH: You've never thought about it? [*Pause.*] We never know where God will lead us.

SHAFANA: Like where?

SARRINAH: Like, I could be the new Nigella.

> *She strikes a pose.*

SHAFANA: The Afghan Australian Nigella?

SARRINAH: And what's so impossible about that?

SHAFANA: Nothing, except you're a highly qualified mechanical engineer.

SARRINAH: Oh, you know this, do you?

SHAFANA: Of course I know this.

SARRINAH: I thought you might have forgotten it, since you couldn't be bothered coming with me to get the badge.

SHAFANA: Can I see?

> SARRINAH *shows her the university laminate. She has it under her clothes.*

Camilla Ah Kin (left) as Sarrinah and Sheridan Harbridge as Shafana in the 2009 Alex Buzo Company production in Sydney. (Photo: Heidrun Löhr)

SARRINAH: I don't think the photo looks like me but apparently that takes years of experience to achieve, what with photography being so clear these days.

SHAFANA: [*laughing*] I think it looks great.

SARRINAH: Why are you laughing?

SHAFANA: Why are you still wearing it?

SARRINAH: This from she who could not be bothered.

SHAFANA: Are you going to wear it to bed as well?

SARRINAH: That would be my business.

SHAFANA: I will have to ask my uncle.

SARRINAH: He is having dinner with your family. Aatifa and her brother are with *Mommon Bozorg*. [*Beat.*] So we can talk.

SHAFANA: I brought a present for Aatifa.

> *She hands her a diaphanous long sleeve top.*

From Dotti. Their fashions this year are fantastic.

SARRINAH: At the shops this week. Shafana has a white handbag. I would like a white handbag.

> *They laugh.*

I can't afford Aatifa to see you anymore. I never know what she might want next.

SHAFANA: A blog site.

SARRINAH: Precisely. [*Beat.*] So.

> *Pause.*

SHAFANA: Today. It was not because I couldn't be bothered.

SARRINAH: Did you get it finished?

SHAFANA: My assignment?

SARRINAH: No, your maiden speech to parliament.

SHAFANA: I still have a way to go.

SARRINAH: So I'm surprised you didn't cancel dinner.

SHAFANA: I love your *Quabili*.

SARRINAH: And?

SHAFANA: And your *bolaanee*.

SARRINAH: And what is wrong with my *sabzi*?

SHAFANA: Nothing. I love your *sabzi*.

SARRINAH: So?

> *Pause.*

SHAFANA: I did need to do some more work on my assignment but that was not the main reason I didn't come with you.

SARRINAH *looks at her.*

You know that I have been re-connecting with my faith in the last year.

SARRINAH: God be praised.

SHAFANA: It wasn't until I started investigating Islam, you know, after 2001, that I realised I wasn't satisfied at the deepest level that I could be. It was only when I went back to the source that I found this sense of serenity that I had never experienced before. I'm going to exhaust this word but to me it is inexhaustible, everything suddenly has meaning.

SARRINAH: He put you in the seed of his eyes.

SHAFANA: Yes. And now I have been seized with the desire to do something.

SARRINAH: Seized?

SHAFANA: I would describe it like that. I have been considering something and the more I consider it the more I would like to do it.

SARRINAH: What?

SHAFANA: I want to be able to discuss it with you because I'm just considering. I honestly have not come to a decision about it.

SARRINAH: Shafana.

SHAFANA: I want to put on the *hijab*.

Pause.

SARRINAH: *Hijab* is an Arabic word. Meaning partition. We are not Arabs. We are Persians.

SHAFANA: What do you think?

SARRINAH: This is an option for all Muslim women. Down the trail.

SHAFANA: Yes.

SARRINAH: You want to do this as a mark of your spiritual awakening?

SHAFANA: [*surprised*] Yes.

SARRINAH: Why are you surprised?

SHAFANA: I'm not.

SARRINAH: You sounded surprised that I would say that.

Pause.

SHAFANA: I wasn't sure if you would understand.

SARRINAH: Do you think I am not a good Muslim because I don't wear the scarf?

SHAFANA: No.

SARRINAH: Do you think you will be a better Muslim than me if you wear the scarf?

SHAFANA: No. No, that's not it. Please.

SARRINAH: Of course I understand what this is about. This response makes me question if *you* understand what this is about…

SHAFANA: I wanted to discuss it.

SARRINAH: To discuss it or to persuade me?

SHAFANA: To discuss it.

SARRINAH: You have already talked about it with your parents?

SHAFANA: Yes.

SARRINAH: And?

SHAFANA: Mum said that she had been contemplating on it for the past five years but had never taken the step to do it. Dad asked me if I was sure of what I was doing. Had I thought about all the consequences, all the things that are going on around the world, all the employment considerations.

SARRINAH: But if you really feel it in your heart these are not reasons not to do it.

SHAFANA: That's right.

SARRINAH: And is that how you feel?

SHAFANA: I want to make real the change that has happened to me, that God really is there and I believe that.

SARRINAH: Okay.

She continues cooking.

SHAFANA: So what do you think?

SARRINAH: It is not my decision. It is nothing to do with me. It is to do with you and God.

Pause.

SHAFANA: People think that you do it because you have been inculcated, you are weak and you have no choice, but for me it is quite the opposite.

SARRINAH: Do you care what people think?

SHAFANA: No.

SARRINAH: Not at all?

SHAFANA: No.

SARRINAH: But you feel that you will have to be brave to put it on?

SHAFANA: Yes, in a way.

SARRINAH: In what way?

SHAFANA: I think that some people will stare at me more because of it. I think that in some ways it can be seen as a symbol of something… some misunderstanding about who I am. I think that people will see the scarf first instead of me.

SARRINAH: Or it could bring more focus on your inner thoughts and who you are as a person. No longer are you a pretty girl or an ugly girl, all those superficial judgments are made irrelevant. It may liberate the inner you to be more prominent.

SHAFANA: Do you think that?

SARRINAH: Do you? [*Pause.*] So you didn't want to come with me today because you want to get your ID card photo taken with the scarf.

SHAFANA: If that is what I decide to do.

SARRINAH: By tomorrow.

SHAFANA: What?

SARRINAH: You told me that you called them and they can fit you in tomorrow.

> *Pause.*

SHAFANA: I can call them again.

SARRINAH: But you probably won't need to.

SHAFANA: What?

SARRINAH: Because you have already made up your mind, haven't you?

SHAFANA: Well. You don't seem to mind.

SARRINAH: What difference would that have made?

SHAFANA: You're my aunt, I love you, I've always looked up to you.

SARRINAH: But this has nothing to do with that, does it?

SHAFANA: No. Of course not.

SARRINAH: So.

> *Pause.*

SHAFANA: Why are you being like this?

SARRINAH: Like what?

SHAFANA: Well, I can tell that you don't want me to do this. But you won't say.

SARRINAH: Are you majoring in mind reading now? Have they added that to the list of your tutorial subjects?

SHAFANA: No.

SARRINAH: Then how can you say I don't want you to do this?

SHAFANA: Because you're being sarcastic about mind reading and you don't usually speak to me like that.

SARRINAH: I'm sorry, Shafana, but if you were looking for an adolescent wall of expectations to rebel against you're not going to find it here.

Pause.

SHAFANA: Is that what you think this is about?

SARRINAH: No, of course not. This is a serious, serious contemplation of the role of God in your life and the expression of your faith and I am not treating it as anything else.

SHAFANA: Be careful that your toe does not go into your eye.

SARRINAH: Ah, so you are also now using our Persian sayings.

SHAFANA: Of course.

Pause.

SARRINAH: So how would you say I have forgotten to get some fresh coriander for the *sabzi*?

SHAFANA: I love your *sabzi*.

SARRINAH: We don't have to have the *sabzi*.

Pause.

SHAFANA: Why don't I go and get some?

SARRINAH: No. Let's forget it.

SHAFANA: I'm happy to go. Do you need anything else?

SARRINAH: No. Please don't bother. There are plenty of other things to eat.

SHAFANA: I'll do this for you. To make up for today.

SARRINAH: You will bring me a posy of fresh herbs?

SHAFANA: I'll be back soon.

SARRINAH: Are you sure?

SHAFANA: Sure.

SARRINAH: Drive carefully.

SHAFANA *leaves.*

When I was in Kabul I was the chief engineer on all government building projects. Not the head of my department. The head of the Institute. Yes. I had achieved a very high rank. The top of my profession. And I did not want to leave my country. But when they dropped a bomb on my daughter's childcare we knew we must leave. My qualifications meant that we got into Australia straight away, before my brother and sisters. I have three sisters who are doctors and a sister who is a geneticist, but they took me immediately. We are a family who prize education. But for my qualifications... I only had photocopies. The government kept the originals so that we would not leave. When I took my papers in Australia the employers were always suspicious. Where are the originals? I would explain. They would nod. Eventually I got a job on a project. But I did not... last. I wanted to get back my papers. The language of engineering, I would do it in English. And so it was that I went back to university just as my Shafana was undertaking her own studies.

Flashback: 2002. University library. SARRINAH *holds a folder with an essay in it.*

I've looked at your assignment.

SHAFANA: Thank you.

SARRINAH: Why is it printed in blue?

SHAFANA: What?

SARRINAH: In blue ink. Why is it printed in blue ink?

SHAFANA: People use blue pens. I thought I could use blue ink.

SARRINAH: You should change it to black. Most people use black.

SHAFANA: I wanted to use blue.

SARRINAH: So this is an arts elective?

SHAFANA: Yes. Wait. I need to go back to the blue thing.

SARRINAH: You want your work to distinguish itself on its own merit. Not because it's blue.

SHAFANA: How does it being blue make any difference to its merit?

SARRINAH: It's convention. It's accepted. This is the final year of your degree, do you want my advice?

SHAFANA: Yes.

SARRINAH: People in the arts have the veneer of difference but at heart they are deeply conservative. Print it in black.

SHAFANA: Right.

SARRINAH: So the subject is contemporary crisis in religion and you've chosen to look at Islam.

SHAFANA: You could choose whatever you wanted to do. It's worth ninety percent of the weight.

SARRINAH: That doesn't give me much faith in your lecturer.

SHAFANA: Why not?

SARRINAH: Because to make something worth ninety percent weight means they only want to mark one assignment.

SHAFANA: Or they want you to concentrate all your attention on one well-researched piece.

SARRINAH: Why does a biology student need to look at comparative religion?

SHAFANA: It's an option.

SARRINAH: So why Islam?

SHAFANA: We are Muslims.

SARRINAH: Yes, but we do not need to prove that to anyone else.

SHAFANA: What?

SARRINAH: Everyone from our country is Muslim. We are practising. This is nothing special to us.

SHAFANA: Yes, but I went into the primary sources.

SARRINAH: You are reading the Qur'an?

SHAFANA: I am reading specific explicit verses of mercies, insight, knowledge and understanding. The scope and the breadth and the depth of Islam is overwhelming, so much connecting to me, and it's like answering one of the most profound questions that I have been asking all this time. Aunt, all at one go it just made me literally ecstatic.

SARRINAH: Yes, it reads like that.

SHAFANA: Like what?

SARRINAH: Like someone who is caught up in a state of emotion rather than reason.

SHAFANA: It has been a faith experience for me.

SARRINAH: Faith can be many things. It can be discipline and observance and consistency.

SHAFANA: For me it was as if a switch had been lit [*clicking her fingers*] and light came in, illuminating my world. Before I was merely seeking for enjoyment and happiness.

SARRINAH: Enjoyment and happiness are not to be downgraded.

SHAFANA: But they are not enough.

SARRINAH: No, because you still must work to make your argument logical.

SHAFANA: Aunt, forget the assignment for a moment.

SARRINAH: You asked me to look at your assignment.

SHAFANA: Yes, but I am trying to tell you what has been happening to me. Education is no longer getting a degree, getting your PhD and that's it, and then one day, when you die, that's it. The value of education is that... it's getting spiritual here... but education illuminated not only my mind and my heart but it reinforced the manifestation of the artist in this world and it even qualified why I should educate myself in all the sciences. I had this... wow level. I'm still at this wow level. I guess it will plateau off at some point but I am still at this wow level, awe-struck by things around me. Appreciation has come in, contentment has come in.

SARRINAH: I have noticed... some changes in you.

SHAFANA: I have started to do the fasts that are required and the prayers.

SARRINAH: We have always done these things.

SHAFANA: Not regularly. Not all of them.

SARRINAH: No, not regularly, not all of them, but still we have done them.

SHAFANA: Yes, of course.

   Pause.

SARRINAH: You cannot expect... that because you have... been moved... that that is relevant to your academic work.

SHAFANA: Last September. The eleventh.

SARRINAH: Changed the world, not the academy.

SHAFANA: But I do not believe it is a holy war.

SARRINAH: Don't get into that.

SHAFANA: But I don't. This killing people, this one human being doing such things to another.

SARRINAH: Be careful.

SHAFANA: This is not Islam.

SARRINAH: Don't open it up.

SHAFANA: But it's not.

SARRINAH: You are not an Imam.

SHAFANA: I am a believer.

SARRINAH: But we are not theologians.

SHAFANA: But I read it myself. Specific verses of mercies, insight, compassion, kindness.

SARRINAH: But that is not what your assignment is asking of you. It is asking you to analyse the crisis, analyse the discourse around it, compare and contrast various points of view, summarise, and provide a lucid overview.

SHAFANA: But what do you think?

SARRINAH: Am I a recognised scholar? Is there an article of mine which can be quoted in your footnotes? No. So what I think does not come into it.

SHAFANA: But what do you think? In yourself? In your own mind?

SARRINAH: I think you are smart and intelligent and you have the potential to go to the very top. I think you are the first grandchild so you are very special for everybody. You must know how special you are to my Aatifa. There are twenty-six grandchildren in the family and you are the role model. How you handle your life is… an example.

> SHAFANA *takes the essay from* SARRINAH.

SHAFANA: So you think I should do another draft?

SARRINAH: I do.

> *The lights change.*

> SHAFANA *enters. She is carrying a bunch of fresh coriander.*

SHAFANA: Here it is.

SARRINAH: Was it busy?

SHAFANA: There were people. It wasn't busy.

SARRINAH: You took a while.

> *Pause.*

SHAFANA: There was traffic.

SARRINAH: I wonder why. At this time of night.

SHAFANA: Perhaps there was an accident.

SARRINAH: Did you see an accident?

SHAFANA: No.

SARRINAH: No. That would be upsetting. [*Pause.*] I don't like to go to that supermarket. It's where your uncle used to clean. When I go, still I see him there. Bent over, sweeping under somebody's feet.

SHAFANA: He has a better job now.

SARRINAH: Yes, but I am haunted by the image of him there. [*Pause.*] Who served you on the checkout?

SHAFANA: What do you mean?

SARRINAH: Was it a girl or a boy?

SHAFANA: A girl.

SARRINAH: They have boys on checkouts now. They are no more or less rude than the girls. Perhaps they do a course. Mostly very young boys. It is their first job. You do not see men on the checkout, like you sometimes see older women. No. By then the boys have moved on. [*Beat.*] But you had a girl.

SHAFANA: Yes.

SARRINAH: Was she wearing a headscarf?

SHAFANA: Is this your way of saying something about my employment prospects?

SARRINAH: No. I have not seen many checkout girls wearing a headscarf, that's all.

SHAFANA: She was not wearing a headscarf.

SARRINAH: No, that would have delayed you.

SHAFANA: Why?

SARRINAH: You might have wanted to speak to her.

SHAFANA: I do not need to speak to every woman who wears the scarf.

> *Pause.*

SARRINAH: What do you want to do?

SHAFANA: I think maybe teach.

SARRINAH: In an Islamic school?

SHAFANA: Or not.

SARRINAH: Have you ever applied for a job?

SHAFANA: You know I haven't.

SARRINAH: Would you fudge the truth to get a job?

SHAFANA: I might.

SARRINAH: Fake your CV?

SHAFANA: I don't think so.

SARRINAH: Lie?

SHAFANA: No.

SARRINAH: I have told baldfaced lies. At an interview they asked me about operating systems and software. In Kabul I could redesign any software system, I could have designed a PC to fly to Mars and collect soil samples. But, you know, I had been out of the profession for a couple of years. There had been updates and features that were unfamiliar. In truth, I didn't know this software at all. As the Australians say, 'It was all Greek to me'. When they asked, I put on my face. 'Of course I know.' The first day I went there they show me my room, say that's your office, no-one is around, I take a deep breath. In the morning the boss was giving me a list of jobs that have to be done and I was closing my door and finishing my work quickly and spending the rest of the time teaching myself how their whole operating and software system worked. I had no lunchtime, no break, I was just constantly sitting and learning. I trusted in my brain.

SHAFANA: You have a good brain.

SARRINAH: On that we both agree.

> *They begin to eat.*

SHAFANA: And so do I.

SARRINAH: Now we are agreeing more often.

SHAFANA: And I don't think that the scarf will have any effect on my ability to get a job.

SARRINAH: And if there was a special school you wanted.

SHAFANA: There isn't.

SARRINAH: I know what it is like to want something so much that you spend your nights crying and your days in despair.

SHAFANA: When you were packing hardware supplies.

SARRINAH: When I was packing hardware supplies.

SHAFANA: So you're a snob.

SARRINAH: And you're a stupid girl.

SHAFANA: What?

SARRINAH: You're a stupid, ignorant girl who doesn't know what it is like to make your way in a country where you didn't go to school.

SHAFANA: I was joking.

SARRINAH: It was not funny.

SHAFANA: Okay. I take it back.

SARRINAH: I am educated. I can't help that. I can't take that back. [*Beat.*] Look at me.

> SHAFANA *looks at her.*

Do you believe me?

> SHAFANA *nods.*

Do you believe that I love you like my own daughter?

SHAFANA: Of course.

SARRINAH: We have a special relationship.

SHAFANA: Yes.

SARRINAH: Because you know that you are not your father's apple-in-the-eye.

Pause.

SHAFANA: That's not true. My father loves me.

SARRINAH: That's not what I said. You know your father loves you. You just don't think you're his favourite. But you know you're mine.

SHAFANA: Everyone else in the family thinks that because I'm…

SARRINAH: Assertive. Articulate.

SHAFANA: Self-sufficient. They forget to encourage me.

SARRINAH: I know.

SHAFANA: It's like my other aunts… I dunno… forget to get excited about things I do. They just expect me to do well and never… applaud me when I do.

SARRINAH: I know.

SHAFANA: And you're not like that. You're…

SARRINAH: Excitable.

SHAFANA: Yes. Young at heart.

SARRINAH: Oh, please. And you were doing so well.

SHAFANA: Well, you are. I love that about you. Even when I'm scared of you I love that about you.

SARRINAH: Scared of me? You're not scared of me, or that would have delayed you. Coming back to speak to me.

Pause.

SHAFANA: Aunt. Please. Just say it. Just say you have major issues. Just scream at me if you are going to.

SARRINAH: Scream what?

SHAFANA: I don't know. Are you crazy? Are you out of your mind, what are you thinking? Why are you doing this?

Pause.

SARRINAH: The coriander is good.

SHAFANA: Yes.

SARRINAH: Much fresher than I have ever tasted in my life before I came here.

SHAFANA: Okay.

SARRINAH: Not just fresher but a different taste, you know what I mean, the soil and the air, all make it taste different. People are crazy if they say that they can make traditional Afghan food here. The food here tastes of Australia.

SHAFANA: But it carries traditions from our homeland.

SARRINAH: You are Australian.

SHAFANA: I am also Afghani.

SARRINAH: Do you want to return to Afghanistan?

SHAFANA: It's a war zone.

SARRINAH: When you went travelling to America you were homesick for Australia.

SHAFANA: Oi, oi, oi.

SARRINAH: Last week you took the train into the city, into the street they call Little Thai Town. You went to the Chat Thai where all the groovy young things go.

SHAFANA *laughs*.

What?

SHAFANA: Groovy young things.

SARRINAH: Well. What do you call yourselves?

SHAFANA: We don't. We just hang out. [*Pause.*] I can still go to Thai Town in a scarf. I can still get the train.

SARRINAH: Many women in scarves end up buying cars. Because they get harassed on public transport. My students tell me this.

SHAFANA: So I can drive.

SARRINAH: Everywhere.

SHAFANA: If I have to.

SARRINAH: Or go out in groups.

SHAFANA: Yes.

SARRINAH: In case you get spat on.

SHAFANA: Women not wearing scarves get spat on too.

SARRINAH: That is true. And fear is not a reason not to do something.

SHAFANA: Exactly.

SARRINAH: In fact, sometimes it is more of a reason to do something. It is a reason to be defiant. To show solidarity with your sisters who are being persecuted in this way.

SHAFANA *throws down her napkin*.

SHAFANA: I am not thinking of it for any of those reasons. All you have mentioned is about consequences. I am not motivated by any of that.

SARRINAH: No?

SHAFANA: No. Do you want to hear? Do you want to hear me when I say that I want to put on the scarf because this is who I am and I feel this is what I want to do? It is for me, not for anyone else. One night I was reading the Qur'an and it just occurred to me, I don't even recall what passage or where, and it just occurred to me, 'Why am I not wearing the scarf, what is stopping me?'

> *Pause.*

SARRINAH: What delayed you before?

SHAFANA: What?

SARRINAH: At the shops. You were delayed and it was not because of traffic.

> SHAFANA *pulls a headscarf out of her pocket.* SARRINAH *takes it from her.*

Twice already you have lied to me. You lied why you didn't want to come to have the photograph. You lied why you took some time at the shops. You stopped to buy this scarf.

SHAFANA: I omitted to tell—

SARRINAH: You lied. You are secretive. And then you pour out your heart, in passion, in heartfeeling words, and you think that is enough?

SHAFANA: Stop screaming at me. Why are you screaming at me?

SARRINAH: I don't know you. I don't know this Shafana.

SHAFANA: I am the same. I am still the same Shafana.

SARRINAH: You are not the same. You are... secretive. Omitting.

SHAFANA: You will not be honest with me about why not. [*Pause.*] Before now I thought that I might like to wear it but I just did not know how to bring myself to the point of putting it on. When I was thinking about it I thought I couldn't do it but then I had a feeling that I have to do it. I have to wear it. And it was amazing.

SARRINAH: So again she has lied.

SHAFANA: I am trying to tell you that it was a beautiful moment. A deep, clear moment.

SARRINAH: Because you said you were still thinking about it, but now you tell me you have had a revelation, a revelation of faith.

SHAFANA: Yes, that is it. That is what it felt like.

SARRINAH: Then what anyone else thinks is utterly, utterly irrelevant. I cannot compete with God.

> *She gives her the scarf back. They eat.*

Tell me right now what this is about.

SHAFANA: I've been telling you.

SARRINAH: An outward sign of your faith.

SHAFANA: Yes.

SARRINAH: And what else?

SHAFANA: What else does it need to be?

SARRINAH: Shafana. You are not like that. You know that you don't just run off, with your feelings.

SHAFANA: I haven't just run off.

SARRINAH: Then you have your own doubts?

SHAFANA: I have my own… considerations.

SARRINAH: Of course you do. You can't live in a religious ecstasy. You are smart enough to examine your own motives.

SHAFANA: Are you saying I'm lying?

SARRINAH: We can all deceive ourselves when we want to.

SHAFANA: I'm not… you think that what we say and what we do are different.

SARRINAH: Of course.

SHAFANA: But sometimes what you see is what you get.

SARRINAH: Well, I don't believe you.

SHAFANA: Well, it's true.

SARRINAH: I don't believe that's all there is to it. [*Pause.*] What else is this about?

SHAFANA: Have you heard of the soft revolution?

SARRINAH: No. Or… it's… is it?

SHAFANA: It's young Muslims who reject both extremists and liberals. They… fight… for human rights… for change to the Hadith… There is a project. It could be the most intellectually active period for Islam since the height of scholarship in the Middle Ages.

SARRINAH: And you want to be part of it?

SHAFANA: I don't know. But for them, for some, the veil is a mask in the power struggle against the dictatorship of men.

　　　Pause.

SARRINAH: So there is another reason?

SHAFANA: I… you're twisting it.

SARRINAH: You think you can synthesise Qur'anic values with the twenty-first century?

SHAFANA: Don't you?

　　　Pause.

SARRINAH: You want to participate in a faith that judges others by the rules it fashions.

SHAFANA: What?

SARRINAH: The rules. The outward cladding of piety.

SHAFANA: No.

SARRINAH: Yes. You want to judge my faith.

SHAFANA: I honestly don't.

SARRINAH: My faith is between me and God. The Qur'an speaks directly to me, Sarrinah, today.

SHAFANA: Of course.

SARRINAH: It is a fundamental part of who I am.

SHAFANA: It is all of who I am.

SARRINAH: No. There is faith and there is reason. There is religion and there is civil society. There is belief and there is the law.

SHAFANA: But your faith touches every part of your life.

SARRINAH: No. My faith is private and cultural. But it is not the answer to all the freedoms we have struggled for.

SHAFANA: But how can you say that?

SARRINAH: Because I have seen what your brand of religion can do. I have witnessed what your brand of fanaticism can destroy.

    Pause.

SHAFANA: My brand of fanaticism?

SARRINAH: I love God with all of my heart and all of my soul and all of my strength. And still, I do not think my faith can ever be the sole source of all knowledge.

SHAFANA: I want to cover my hair. That is all.

SARRINAH: That is the beginning.

SHAFANA: No, it's not. How dare you.

SARRINAH: How dare I?

SHAFANA: You sound like some ignorant Australian. This is a matter of faith.

SARRINAH: This is the beginning of subjecting your will.

SHAFANA: Actually it's quite the opposite.

SARRINAH: Shafana. It means letting go of all my hopes for you.

SHAFANA: It doesn't have to.

SARRINAH: You don't know the world.

SHAFANA: I trust in God.

SARRINAH: You think I don't?

SHAFANA: I know you do. Aunt. I know you. Who else have I looked up to? Who taught me to believe in my own desires? It is you who told me to clutch my dreams in my screwed-up fists and carry them into reality. To listen to no counsel so much as the small voice of God who whispers inside my soul.

SARRINAH: Are you reading the newspapers, Shafana?

SHAFANA: I will practise my faith without discrimination.

SARRINAH: And that is what you will spend all your time fighting to assert.

SHAFANA: If I must.

> *Pause.*

SARRINAH: I am glad that we have a chance to talk.

SHAFANA: Yes.

SARRINAH: There is something I also must talk about.

> SHAFANA *continues to eat.*

You know that I have loaned some money to your parents so that you can continue your education. [*Beat*.] I am afraid. It is difficult for me to say, but you know that all around people are having to be more careful with their money.

SHAFANA: Aunt?

SARRINAH: I am going to have to ask your parents to repay that money to us.

SHAFANA: But they do not have the money to repay you.

SARRINAH: Then, and I am sorry, Shafana, you may have to withdraw from your studies. [*Pause.*] Perhaps if you would get a job and defer for one year. If you could show us all that you are able to get along in the real world, as we have had to do.

SHAFANA: Defer my studies? But I have just re-enrolled.

SARRINAH: Think of it merely as an obstacle in your path.

SHAFANA: And this is what you are threatening to do, if I choose to wear the headscarf?

> *Pause.*

SARRINAH: Don't be ridiculous. They have nothing to do with each other. Nothing. It is rudeness for you to suggest that there is any connection.

> SHAFANA *picks up the headscarf and holds it out.*

SHAFANA: Will you put it on me then?

SARRINAH: What?

SHAFANA: You have not uttered a single objection. You have shown nothing but understanding and support. Then will you help me to tie it on?

SARRINAH: You do not need to wear the scarf inside.

SHAFANA: No. But. To try it.

SARRINAH: I have told you. This is between you and God.

SHAFANA: But it would mean a lot to me. My favourite aunt. It would give me courage.

SARRINAH *begins clearing up the dinner things.*

SARRINAH: You will have to have an opinion about everything to do with Muslim Australia.

SHAFANA: Why?

SARRINAH: What do you think about the girls being raped in the Western suburbs?

SHAFANA: Well, what am I supposed to think? It's terrible.

SARRINAH: Yes, but you will have to defend that Islam does not encourage such an act.

SHAFANA: You know that it doesn't.

SARRINAH: Yes, but you will be making yourself a visible symbol. An endless advertisement that says, 'Ask me. Accuse me'. I am not a person but a representative of my faith. I will spend all my time explaining. As if you should be grateful to be tolerated.

SHAFANA: I am not grateful to be tolerated. I'm an Australian citizen. I do not have to ask to be tolerated.

SARRINAH: You think?

SHAFANA: I do not have to ask to be tolerated.

SARRINAH: What world are you living in?

SHAFANA: The free world.

SARRINAH: Wake up.

SHAFANA: You wake up. I do not have to ask to be tolerated.

SARRINAH: In law.

SHAFANA: Yes, in law.

SARRINAH: And in the community?

SHAFANA: It is not as bad as you say. It isn't. Maybe it was, straight after 9/11 but not now. Things are changing. Really changing. Diversity is…

SARRINAH: Tolerated.

SHAFANA: Welcomed. Celebrated.

SARRINAH: Let's see.

> *Pause.*

SHAFANA: I will answer any questions as well as I can. It will give me an opportunity to explain that Islam is not what so many people think.

SARRINAH: What do you think of the Bali bombings? What do you think of the Afghanistan war, the invasion of Iraq, the backwash of 9/11? What do you think of the Taliban and honour killings, what do you think? How can you justify being part of such a religion? And it won't even be that rational. As far as they're concerned you may as well have driven the planes into the towers, you may as well have held the girls down and urged them to be raped.

SHAFANA: Stop it.

SARRINAH: You won't be able to stop it.

SHAFANA: There may be incidents.

SARRINAH: There will be endless, unexpected, irrational incidents. Tiny, tiny sneers and full-throated abuse.

> *Pause.*

SHAFANA: And your way is just to give in?

SARRINAH: You're not listening to me.

SHAFANA: Your solution is just to hide? Fade into the background.

SARRINAH: That's not what I'm saying.

SHAFANA: Assimilate. Disappear into the masses. Never speak up, never stand up. Well, maybe if you'd spoken up in Afghanistan the country wouldn't be in the mess it is in now.

> *Pause.*

SARRINAH: You think the Taliban got into power because moderate Afghanis lost their voice?

SHAFANA: I don't know. You never talk about it. No-one in the family will talk about it.

SARRINAH: It is our way of grieving.

SHAFANA: Well, this is my way of understanding.

SARRINAH: At the National Museum they used sledge hammers to destroy artworks that were deemed blasphemous. At the Kabul zoo the animals were killed or left to starve. In Mazar-i-Sharif and in Bamiyan they shot dead eight thousand people. Then they forbade the corpses to be buried for six days. This is not a story on the evening news. This is what they did. You do not reason with fanatics. You do not argue with zealots. Their whole work is one rule and one law and one way of being.

SHAFANA: They are thugs and bullies.

SARRINAH: When we were escaping through Pakistan, the dealers told us that I had to wear a *chador*, the garment with only one window at the front. We were to get on a bus from Pakistan to India, with me disguised in this *chador*. It was so hot and there were maybe one hundred people packed onto this bus. We had to crawl over other people's legs and bodies to get into the bus. I could hardly breathe. We had to sit with our knees pressed up against the bars on the windows and more and more I was struggling for breath. The window at the front of the *chador* was disappearing, my mouth was covered and I was suffocating on mouthfuls of material. I could not breathe and I thought I was going to die. I thought I was going to be sick. The air was in my throat but wouldn't go down into my lungs, I was suffocating. I was under water, holding my breath until my lungs involuntarily sucked down wads of cotton and I could not breathe. I pulled the front of the garment up to here. And there was a shout. Get off the bus. You. You there. Get off the bus now. Everyone was looking at us. The soldiers were pointing at us. Get off the bus now. They had guns. They were pointing guns at us and they are not small handguns, these are black Russian guns, AK-47s. Get off the bus now. The soldiers had recognised that we were not Pakistani.

Because I lifted up the veil? I don't know. Because the *chador* was whiter than the others on the bus? I don't know. Because of the way I was wearing it, I don't know. They put us in jail. The Pakistani jails have no water. No food. People just go to the toilet anywhere. And now we were going to be sent back to Afghanistan. They drove us to the border, we saw the Afghani flag at the border and that's when the dealers came for us again. They took us back on their ute, we got back on that bus and finally we went through the checkpoint. This took us nine days. With no shower, our clothes were stiff with dirt and the whole time I had to wear this… tent… that…

Pause.

SHAFANA: Why don't you ever talk about it?

SARRINAH: Because I get like this. I don't want to go back there.

SHAFANA: But if the pain is still there.

SARRINAH: This is not an episode of the Oprah show, Shafana. I don't get to tell it all out and then feel better. This is pain carved into the bones of my feet and horror tattooed around the base of my skull. This is not something I use in an argument to make my point.

Pause.

SHAFANA: Will you ever talk to Aatifa about this?

SARRINAH: No.

SHAFANA: She's your daughter.

Pause.

SARRINAH: Tomorrow night I will make *borani banjan* and *salaata* with coriander chutney. Will you come again for dinner?

SHAFANA: No. I don't think so.

SARRINAH: As you like.

Pause.

SHAFANA: Thank you for telling me about your life.

SARRINAH: I told you only about the past.

SHAFANA: I am interested in your past.

SARRINAH: You are too interested in what is past.

SHAFANA: How else can I know who I am?

SARRINAH: You should go out with friends of your own age.

Pause.

SHAFANA: I will have more study to do.

SARRINAH: Yes.

SHAFANA: In fact, I should get back to it now.

SARRINAH: Goodnight then, Shafana.

She kisses her.

SHAFANA: Goodnight, Aunt.

SARRINAH: I will come into your laboratory tomorrow morning.

SHAFANA: Yes, do.

SARRINAH: Before your tutorial.

SHAFANA: Good.

SARRINAH: To hear what you have decided.

SHAFANA *exits.*

In a new country your religion becomes the main focus of how you are being seen, we all go a bit deeper into who we are and where we belong. The society we are living in, we are thinking about how we are going to protect our children, we want it to be in a direction that they are not going to be hurt, not going to be victimised.

Flashback: the aunt's lounge room, 12 September 2001.

SHAFANA *enters.*

Are you—?

SHAFANA: Okay.

SARRINAH: Been—?

SHAFANA: Watching the—

SARRINAH: Yep.

SHAFANA: They keep playing—

SARRINAH: I know.

SHAFANA: The footage—

SARRINAH: Yeah.

SHAFANA: And I keep watching it—

SARRINAH: Me too.

SHAFANA: Even when I've seen it. Like I'm mesmerised by it. I keep watching—

SARRINAH: The planes go in—

SHAFANA: Yeah.

SARRINAH: How did you—?

SHAFANA: When I woke up the radio announcer— And I said to Dad something big's happened. So I turned on the TV and it hasn't been off.

SARRINAH: I can't believe it.

SHAFANA: No. And every time—

SARRINAH: What?

SHAFANA: Every time they say extremists—

SARRINAH: I know.

SHAFANA: Islamic extremists.

SARRINAH: Terrorists.

SHAFANA: And the words get jumbled up and suddenly we're—

SARRINAH: I know.

SHAFANA: [*crying*] I can't believe it.

SARRINAH: Promise me you'll be careful.

SHAFANA: What?

SARRINAH: At your university.

SHAFANA: Careful of what?

SARRINAH: Don't get drawn into arguments.

SHAFANA: What sort of arguments?

SARRINAH: Listen to me, at the site where I'm working they call them 'your lot'.

SHAFANA: They don't like working with a female engineer.

SARRINAH: That's right.

SHAFANA: So even if you weren't Afghani.

SARRINAH: But I am and they know it.

SHAFANA: This won't—

SARRINAH: It will.

SHAFANA: Most people—

SARRINAH: Listen to me. This is something else. This is a whole new—

SHAFANA: But it's got nothing to do with…

SARRINAH: Listen. I'm going to resign.

> *Pause.*

SHAFANA: You're not.

SARRINAH: I am.

SHAFANA: It took you ages to get them to recognise your Afghan credentials here. It took you years to get this job on a project.

SARRINAH: This is not the time.

SHAFANA: You can't. Please tell me you won't do this.

SARRINAH: I have a young daughter. I have a young son.

SHAFANA: Are you being harassed?

SARRINAH: What? No.

SHAFANA: Has a man done something to you? Rubbed up against you?

SARRINAH: No. [*Beat.*] What man has rubbed up against you?

SHAFANA: No-one.

SARRINAH: Tell me.

SHAFANA: You're scared and I know that you don't get scared of anything except… like all women you must get intimidated by their smell and their bullying and—

SARRINAH: There has been no bullying. I want to resign for my own reasons.

SHAFANA: But this is your freedom. You taught me that.

SARRINAH: This is a whole new world order.

SHAFANA: I don't believe you're saying this. I don't believe this is what it's about.

SARRINAH: I'll do a PhD.

SHAFANA: You have a PhD.

SARRINAH: I must redo it. In English, to be able to teach.

SHAFANA: You're being totally paranoid.

SARRINAH: I am totally paranoid.

SHAFANA: You told me yourself. You had a good experience with Australian people. Both of your first bosses really helped you and tried to improve the level that you were at. The reason you have the job is because your Australian boss spoke highly of you.

SARRINAH: That is all true.

SHAFANA: And so?

SARRINAH: Did you see what happened today? Did you see the planes go into the towers? Do you see how the world has changed? [*Pause.*] Look. A woman engineer on an Australian building site. It was never going to be easy. In India, yes, there are many women in building. In Indonesia, many many. In Australia…

SHAFANA: You've never backed down before. [*Beat.*] You've changed.

> *Pause.*

SARRINAH: Yes, I have.

SHAFANA: You're afraid.

SARRINAH: Yes, I am.

SHAFANA: But don't be.

SARRINAH: Just like that? [*Pause.*] Don't judge me, Shafana.

SHAFANA: I'm not.

SARRINAH: We have to listen to the little voice inside. The small, persistent voice of God. He has other plans.

> *Shafana's laboratory.*

> SHAFANA *sings the Dari song 'Taranha Saalang' ('Song of Saalang'). As she sings she puts on the headscarf.*

SHAFANA: *Saalang koh wa darya daarah*
        Darya khroshaan ast

Har so gulestaan ast
Gunjeshk haa safaid wa zard wa sabz paran ast
Bar shaakh-saaraan ast
Maiehan naam-e-tu rashan boohad taa een jahaan ast
Taa een jahaan ast
Saalang maywa daara rang rang tootash feraawaan ast
Darya khroshaan ast
Sheer maahi ba darya mast mastaan raqs raqsaan ast
Maahi feraawaan ast
Maiehan naam-e-tu rashan boohad taa een jahaan asst
Taa een jahaan ast.

SARRINAH *enters and begins to cry.*

BOTH: *Saalang koh wa darya daarah*
Darya khroshaan ast
Har so gulestaan ast
Gunjeshk haa safaid wa zard wa sabz paran ast
Bar shaakh-saaraan ast
Maiehan naam-e-tu rashan boohad taa een jahaan ast
Taa een jahaan ast.

SARRINAH *puts a jar before* SHAFANA.

SHAFANA: What's that?

SARRINAH *is increasingly upset.*

SARRINAH: It's ah… it's dried shrimp put in… ah… water.

SHAFANA: Dried shrimp?

SARRINAH: You can buy them in Chinatown.

SHAFANA: They still look really shrivelled.

SARRINAH: I was working with limited… I had to go down to one of the Chinatown supermarkets and I couldn't get a park and… look they're shrivelled up, okay?

SHAFANA: Why have you got a jar of shrivelled-up shrimp?

SARRINAH: [*very upset now*] Well, obviously because the Chinese don't freeze-dry metre-and-a-half tube worms.

SHAFANA: Aunt.

SARRINAH: Don't do this.

SHAFANA: It's done.

SARRINAH: You can just take it off. No-one will know. Just take it off.

Pause.

SHAFANA: You think I'm going to shrivel?

SARRINAH: I want you to see it can happen.

SHAFANA: You went to Chinatown and bought dried shrimp and you put them in a jar?

SARRINAH: Yes. Yes, alright. I wanted you to look at them.

SHAFANA: That's not going to happen to me.

SARRINAH: Look at them. Please.

SHAFANA: You can't ask me to do this.

SARRINAH: For me.

SHAFANA: No.

SARRINAH: I'm begging you.

SHAFANA: You don't beg.

SARRINAH: I will.

SHAFANA: You don't beg.

SARRINAH: If I beg will you not do it?

Camilla Ah Kin (left) as Sarrinah and Sheridan Harbridge as Shafana in the 2009 Alex Buzo Company production in Sydney. (Photo: Heidrun Löhr)

Pause.

SHAFANA: No.

    SARRINAH *cries.*

SARRINAH: I wanted you to have freedom.

SHAFANA: I do. I have this freedom.

SARRINAH: No.

SHAFANA: Yes. This is the freedom I have.

A long, long pause.

SARRINAH: Congratulations then.

SHAFANA: Thank you.

SARRINAH: A Muslim woman can do anything. She can be an academic. She can be anything. Anything.

SHAFANA: Of course.

SARRINAH: You have chosen to fulfil something else in your life now. This is very satisfying for you.

SHAFANA: Aunt.

Camilla Ah Kin (foreground) as Sarrinah and Sheridan Harbridge as Shafana in the 2009 Alex Buzo Company production in Sydney. (Photo: Heidrun Löhr)

SARRINAH: Yes.

> SHAFANA *takes both* SARRINAH's *hands in hers.*

You are stronger.

SHAFANA: Since I put on my cape.

SARRINAH: Your what?

SHAFANA: The husband of my friend. He describes it as her Superman cape.

SARRINAH: And is that how it feels?

> *Pause.*

SHAFANA: Will you come with me to have my photo taken?

> *A long pause.*

SARRINAH: But where will we find a wig?

SHAFANA: A wig?

SARRINAH: In Turkish universities women are given the choice between removing their scarf and wearing a wig.

SHAFANA: Do you think I am going to study in Turkey?

SARRINAH: Well, I don't know what you might do. But I am talking about now.

SHAFANA: I do not need a wig.

SARRINAH: Well, if you are going to get your photo taken, so. I should get a new card also.

SHAFANA: You want to put on… the wig?

SARRINAH: I thought I could have one card as Doctor of Mechanical Engineering and one as the Afghan/Australian Nigella.

> *Pause.*

SHAFANA: You think I should get two cards?

SARRINAH: In case you change your mind.

SHAFANA: I won't change my mind.

SARRINAH: I know. On our path, we choose.

SHAFANA: Yes.

SARRINAH: Yes. And now I was having a joke with you.

SHAFANA: A joke?

> *She smacks* SARRINAH *playfully on the arm.*

This is not a joking matter. This is a serious matter.

> *But she is laughing.*

SARRINAH: And so is cooking. Cooking is the most serious matter.

SHAFANA: Then perhaps *I* will become the Afghan/Australian Nigella.

SARRINAH: It could double as a tea towel.

SHAFANA: Aunt!

They embrace.

SARRINAH: I will miss you.

SHAFANA: I am still the same.

SARRINAH: Then I will miss your hair.

SHAFANA *smacks her on the arm again.*

SHAFANA: You have learnt bad habits in Australia.

SARRINAH: I do not understand this saying 'taking the piss'.

SHAFANA: Oh, I think you understand it very well.

SARRINAH: But whose… er… piss… are you supposed to be stealing?

SHAFANA: Taking. You are taking it.

SARRINAH: But where are you taking it?

SHAFANA: I don't know.

SARRINAH: And why would you want someone else's…?

SHAFANA: Aunt.

SARRINAH: Do you think it means making someone laugh so much that they… are urinating in their pants?

SHAFANA: I think so.

SARRINAH: And this is good? In Australia?

SHAFANA: Are you sure this is what you want to talk about?

SARRINAH: You are the eldest Aussie grandchild. These are the things you should be able to speak about with the knowledge.

SHAFANA: As you wish.

SARRINAH: Yes. [*Pause.*] Before I go.

SHAFANA: What?

SARRINAH: Have you mentioned to your parents?

SHAFANA: Will you still be needing back your loan?

Pause.

SARRINAH: *Khak da sahrem.* What kind of dirt should I put on my head?

SHAFANA: I said nothing of it to my—

SARRINAH: I… could not. [*Beat.*] I thought I was in a Bollywood film maybe or a BBC television.

SHAFANA: The world is in a lot of trouble.

SARRINAH: We are family. We will find a way.

SHAFANA: And I would rather you cut your teeth on me.

SARRINAH: Cut my teeth?

SHAFANA: Practised on me.

SARRINAH: Practised for what?

SHAFANA: For when you come to talk to Aatifa about it.

> *Pause.*

SARRINAH: Aatifa?

SHAFANA: …

SARRINAH: My daughter?

SHAFANA: She told me she didn't like the attention she was getting about her appearance.

SARRINAH: She is in Year Seven.

SHAFANA: She doesn't like the compliments.

SARRINAH: She is thirteen years old.

SHAFANA: I told her she should wait.

SARRINAH: She will wait. No. She is not allowed to even think about putting on the scarf.

SHAFANA: She sees other young girls.

SARRINAH: No. No.

SHAFANA: She should wait.

SARRINAH: When she is eighteen or nineteen or twenty, then she can consider.

SHAFANA: I agree.

SARRINAH: You agree?

> *Pause.*

SHAFANA: I will tell her that myself. Although, if she really wants to do it I couldn't, in good faith, stop her. I mean, she is young but who am I to say at what age she can make such a decision if she really has thought it through? Still, I will advise her to wait.

SARRINAH: When will you do that?

SHAFANA: What do you mean?

SARRINAH: You won't be seeing her again.

> *Pause.*

SHAFANA: You can't.

SARRINAH: Can't?

SHAFANA: That won't stop her.

SARRINAH: We'll see.

SHAFANA: Why are you doing this?

SARRINAH: Because. Today you and I become…

SHAFANA: Not enemies.

SARRINAH: Opponents. You are my opponent now.

SHAFANA: I don't want to be your opponent.

SARRINAH: Still.

SHAFANA: What does that mean, to be your opponent?

> SARRINAH *takes a scarf out of her pocket.*

Are you going to tear it in half?

> SARRINAH *shakes her head.*

Are you going to tear it off my head?

SARRINAH: No, we don't do that.

SHAFANA: So we just agree to disagree?

> SARRINAH *takes the scarf and lifts it over her head. As if to put it on. Then she wraps it around her neck, then ties or pins it in place.*

SARRINAH: You and I are not 'we' anymore.

SHAFANA: Yes we are.

> SARRINAH *puts her hand up to* SARRINAH*'s face.*

SARRINAH: [*gently*] No. We're not. Not because I don't want to be, just because we aren't.

SHAFANA: I don't want to be… [*She is crying.*] I love you.

SARRINAH: I love you too. That's not… we choose.

SHAFANA: So from today I won't see you?

SARRINAH: You'll see me. I'll see you. But we won't be able to… see each other.

SHAFANA: Why are you being so ruthless?

SARRINAH: We can pretend. We can pretend that this is a disagreement about… oh, I don't know… what TV chef we like best. Let's pretend it's just like that. And say… nothing. But, deeply, I am opposed to the path you advocate. Now.

SHAFANA: We can find other points of agreement.

SARRINAH: This from the girl who has just made such a choice.

> *Pause.*

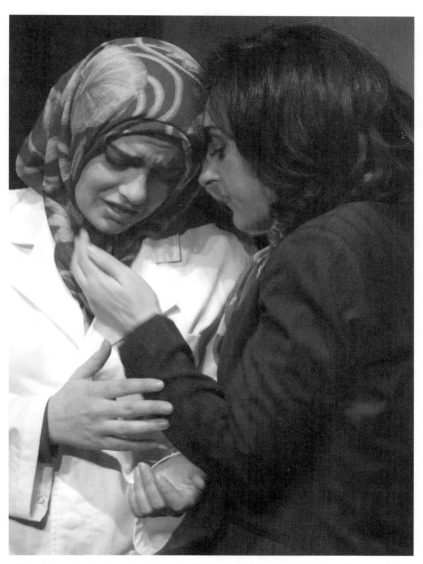

Sheridan Harbridge (left) as Shafana and Camilla Ah Kin as Sarrinah in the 2009 Alex Buzo Company production in Sydney. (Photo: Heidrun Löhr)

SHAFANA: Opponents?

SARRINAH: Yes.

SHAFANA: It sounds so… I don't know.

SARRINAH: Adult?

SARRINAH *kisses her on the forehead and exits.*

SHAFANA: I am thinking about the mussels that live in total darkness in seas that are filled with brine. I am focussing on the way in which they carefully cling to the edges of pools that would kill them in an instant. I am mindful of their precarious determination. I am inspired by their shrugging off of the demands of this endless, toughest balancing act of all. In the deep undersea, there are such creatures, and there are yet new worlds to be fathomed and new impossibilities to be revealed.

THE END

www.currency.com.au

Visit the Currency Press website to:

- Buy your books online
- Browse through our full list of titles, from plays to screenplays, books on theatre, film and music, and more
- Choose a play for your school or amateur performance group by cast size and gender
- Obtain information about performance rights
- Find out about theatre productions and other performing arts news across Australia
- For students, read our study guides
- For teachers, access syllabus and other relevant information
- Sign up for our email newsletter

The performing arts publisher